Facts About the Fly

By Lisa Strattin

© 2019 Lisa Strattin

Facts for Kids Picture Books by Lisa Strattin

Little Blue Penguin, Vol 92

Chipmunk, Vol 5

Frilled Lizard, Vol 39

Blue and Gold Macaw, Vol 13

Poison Dart Frogs, Vol 50

Blue Tarantula, Vol 115

African Elephants, Vol 8

Amur Leopard, Vol 89

Sabre Tooth Tiger, Vol 167

Baboon, Vol 174

Sign Up for New Release Emails Here

http://LisaStrattin.com/subscribe-here

Monthly Surprise Box

http://KidCraftsByLisa.com

IMAGES

Contents

INTRODUCTION 7

CHARACTERISTICS 9

APPEARANCE 11

LIFE STAGES 13

LIFE SPAN 15

SIZE 17

HABITAT 19

DIET 21

ENEMIES 23

SUITABILITY AS PETS 25

PLUSH FLY TOY 38

MONTHLY SURPRISE BOX 39

INTRODUCTION

The fly, more specifically, the housefly, is one of the most common and well-known insects in the world and is found everywhere.

CHARACTERISTICS

There are more than 240,000 different species of fly worldwide but only around half of these have are presumed to actually have been scientifically documented.

APPEARANCE

The housefly, the most common fly species found in houses. Adults are grey to black, with four dark, longitudinal lines on the thorax, slightly hairy bodies, and a single pair of membranous wings. They have red eyes, these are set farther apart in the slightly larger female.

LIFE STAGES

Each female housefly can lay up to 500 eggs in her lifetime, in batches of about 75 to 150 at a time. The eggs are white and are about .05 inches in length, deposited by the fly in a suitable place, usually dead and decaying organic matter, such as food waste, carrion, or feces.

Within a day, maggots hatch from the eggs; living and feeding where they were laid. The magots then crawl to a dry, cool place and transform into pupae for the next life stage. In about 20 days, the adult fly emerges from the pupa, and begins its life of being a nuisance to people and animals.

14

LIFE SPAN

Flies have an extremely short lifespan, only living for about one month.

16

SIZE

Flies average between 1/5th to just over 1 inch long, depending on the particular species.

18

HABITAT

The housefly is probably the insect with the widest distribution in the world; it has accompanied humans around the globe. It is found in the Arctic Circle, as well as in the tropics, where it is abundant. It is present in all populated parts of Europe, Asia, Africa, Australasia, and the Americas.

DIET

Flies are omnivorous animals and will eat almost anything from the nectar of plants, to sap, and even animal blood. The fly is able to prey on these because it uncoils it's long, straw-like tongue in order to suck the liquid into the fly's body. Maggots, which are the baby flies, feed primarily on decomposing matter such as excrement and flesh.

ENEMIES

Due to its small size and abundance, the fly is preyed upon by a wide variety of predators around the world including amphibians such as frogs, toads and newts. There are fish that eat flies that land on the surface of the water. Many reptiles such as lizards and small mammals also eat them.

SUITABILITY AS PETS

Flies are not known to be pets. Since they are mostly a nuisance to people, they are commonly killed when we can get close enough to kill them.

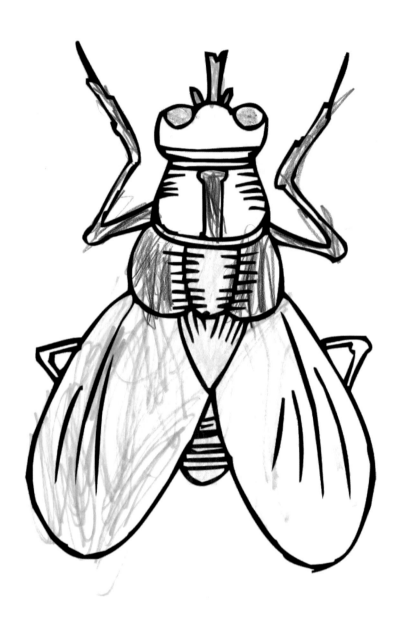

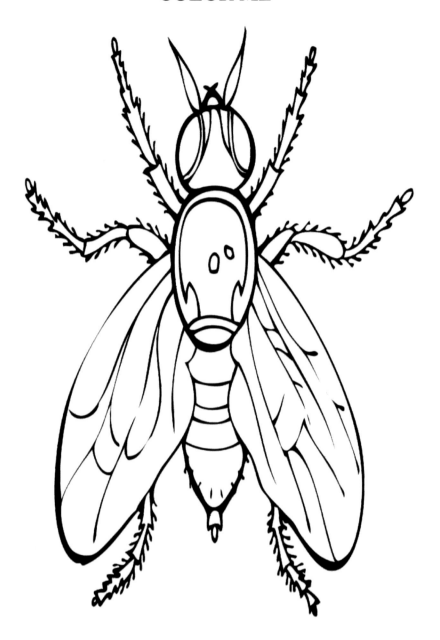

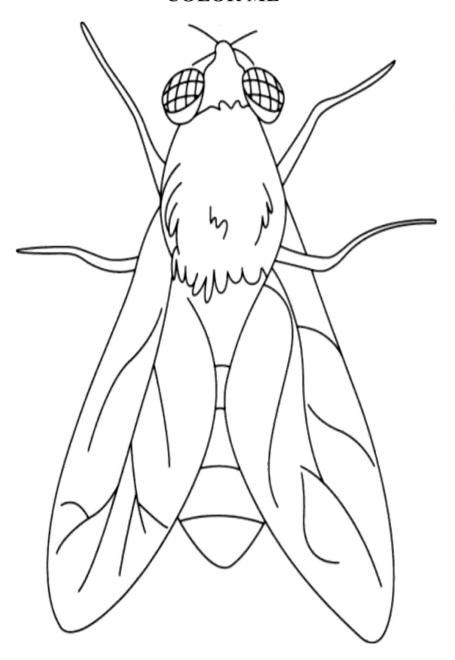

COLOR ME

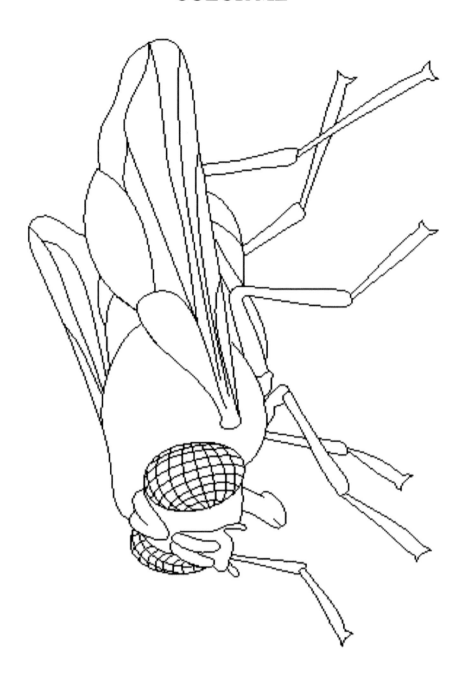

Please leave me a review here:

http://lisastrattin.com/Review-Vol-246

For more Kindle Downloads Visit Lisa Strattin Author Page on Amazon Author Central

http://amazon.com/author/lisastrattin

To see upcoming titles, visit my website at LisaStrattin.com– all books available on kindle!

http://lisastrattin.com

PLUSH FLY TOY

You can get one by copying and pasting this link into your browser:

http://lisastrattin.com/PlushFly

MONTHLY SURPRISE BOX

Get yours by copying and pasting this link into your browser

http://KidCraftsByLisa.com

Made in the USA
Las Vegas, NV
20 May 2021